D0842624

Published in Great Britain by National Portrait Gallery Publications,
National Portrait Gallery, St Martin's Place, London WC2H 0HE

ISBN 1 85514 201 5

A catalogue record for this book is available from the British Library

Series Project Editors: Gillian Forrester and Lucy Clark
Series Picture Researcher: Susie Foster
Series Designer: Karen Osborne
Printed by PJ Reproductions, London

Front cover
George Gordon Byron, Lord Byron, 1788–1824
Thomas Phillips, 1835, after the portrait of 1813 (detail)
Oil on canvas, 76.5 x 63.9cm
© National Portrait Gallery (142)

For a complete catalogue of current publications,
please write to the address above.

CONTENTS

❧

INTRODUCTION

❧

What is a Romantic poet *supposed* to look like? One answer is simply – like Lord Byron: beautiful, brooding and damned. Byron's image – the dark, curly locks, the mocking aristocratic eyes, the voluptuous mouth, the chin with its famous dimple, and the implicit radiation of sexual danger – became famous throughout Britain after the publication of *Childe Harold's Pilgrimage* (1812). By the time of his death in Greece twelve years later it had launched an international style. The dark clothes, the white open-necked shirt exposing the masculine throat, the aggressive display of disarray and devilry, these were the symbols of the Romantic poetic type: the Fallen Angel in rebellion.

Yet if Byron was naturally the beau ideal of the poet, his image was deliberately manufactured and even commercially marketed. He was the most frequently painted poet of his generation: the National Portrait Gallery archives record over forty portraits and miniatures done during his lifetime, as well as several busts, innumerable medallions and 'a wax model from life made by Madame Tussaud in 1816 before her departure for Italy'.

He was also the most self-conscious of subjects. He banned pens or books from his portraits, as being too like 'trade' and not 'spontaneous' enough. ('I am like the tyger (in poesy) if I miss my first spring – I go growling back to my jungle.' [Letter to John Murray, 1820]) His private letters show Byron to have been as anxious about his appearance – his weight, his hair-loss, his club foot, his careful-casual linen – as any modern film star. He was still sending for special tooth powders in the weeks immediately before his death at Missolonghi.

Thomas Phillips's famous portrait of Byron in Albanian soldier's dress, complete with turban, jewel and dagger (featured on the cover of this book), was a deliberate piece of theatrical staging. Sir David Piper has well described it as 'almost Errol Flynn playing Byron'; but it can also be seen as a shrewd commercial publicity shot for the author of *Lara* and *The Corsair*. Byron had bought the costume on his travels in the Epirus (1809), and commissioned the portrait back in London (1813), paying for it out of his royalties. It was a sound long-term investment, as the original eventually went back in triumph to fly the flag at the British Embassy in Athens, while one copy was commissioned as a trophy for his publisher's 'Byron Room', and another was sold to the National Portrait Gallery in 1862.

LORD BYRON, Richard Westall, 1813

LORD BYRON, *by, or after* Richard Westall, 1813 or later

His publisher John Murray skilfully controlled the portraits that were engraved for the frontispieces to his best-selling poems (which frequently sold more than ten thousand copies in a week). Some of these images were immediately 'improved', to conform to the popular expectations of the Romantic bard. In the second version of Westall's 1813 portrait, Byron's eyes were raised apocalyptically to heaven, his hair quiffed and tinted, his brow blanched, his throat swollen with passion, and even his decorative collar-pin altered from a gentleman's cameo to a large, glassy lover's keepsake.

The popular idea of the *inspired* writer, which we now consider an essential aspect of the true poet, has its own particular history. In the mid-eighteenth century, the dominant mode for picturing genius (whether literary or artistic) was still that of the Gentleman at Ease in his Study, often surrounded by the comfortable furnishings of solidly bound books and decorative inkwells. If Inspiration was present, it was usually in the form of an attendant Muse in sportive draperies (tenderly seductive) or as a classical bust (severely instructive), though these according to Horace Walpole should be examples of elegant 'wit' rather than solemn neoclassical 'symbols'.

The striking pair of portraits by Peter Vandyke of Coleridge and Southey, commissioned by the young Bristol publisher Joseph Cottle in 1795, show the two poets as fiery prophets of a new age (see pages 26 and 31). They are wild, they are provocative, they are androgynous, and above all they are *young*. It is no coincidence that they look extraordinarily like the student radicals of the 1960s; or rather, that the student radicals – '*Imagination au pouvoir!*' – looked like them.

This was the time of the great dream of Pantisocracy, when Coleridge and Southey planned to abandon their studies and emigrate to the banks of the Susquehanna river in upper-state Pennsylvania to start European civilisation anew in an ideal American community of equal, self-governing men and women. They were giving public lectures on such revolutionary themes, and their portraits vividly convey the electricity of their youthful presence to an audience, their huge eyes and wildly exaggerated hair (much remarked on at the time by local newspaper reports in Bristol). They express a new kind of dangerous, democratic energy and romantic fervour. The high silk cravats and brightly coloured redingotes are conscious tributes to the current styles in France, where the revolutionary Jacobins were debating the future of mankind in the Paris Convention at the time of the Terror.

When Dorothy Wordsworth first glimpsed Coleridge two years later (characteristically he jumped over a gate and sprinted across a field to meet her) she quoted Shakespeare's definition of a poet: 'He is a wonderful man. His conversation teems with soul, mind and spirit ... His eye is large and full, not dark but grey ... it speaks every emotion of his animated mind; it has more of the 'poet's eye in a fine frenzy rolling' than I ever witnessed.' (*Letters*, 1797)

The circle that formed round Coleridge and Dorothy's brother William over the next decade revolutionised English poetry, and reanimated English prose through the highly personalised essays of Charles Lamb, William Hazlitt and Thomas De Quincey. It also changed forever our idea of creativity and the individual imagination. The Romantic writer was revealed as essentially an inspired autobiographer, drawing on an inner world of experiences going right back into childhood, and now looked upon as to some degree a physical embodiment of his or her own literary work. Hazlitt, himself trained as a painter and aesthetic philosopher, christened this emergent style the 'egotistical Sublime'. Poetry became an impassioned projection of deep autobiography, and the portrait became a further extension of this expanded self: a visual record of mysteriously radiating energies and original genius. The word 'genius' itself began to change its popular meaning around 1800, implying exceptional gifts as opposed to mere technical skill and talent.

So with the next generation, that of Keats, Shelley and John Clare, the portraiture became more intimate and moving. Public confrontation and posing (still inescapable with Byron) was steadily replaced by meditation, and an extraordinary haunting quality of self-reflection and self-awareness. The notion of the poet as the *neglected* genius, doomed to die young or go mad, and remain largely unrecognised by the general public, subtly modulated the pictorial style. There is an extraordinary lack of flamboyance in these later Romantic pictures: no exotic furnishings, or stagey positioning in the Sir Joshua Reynolds idiom; no flashy brushwork or racy silver highlights in the Thomas Gainsborough manner. (Gainsborough sometimes used ground glass to achieve his glittery finishes.) They are quiet, direct, intense.

Many of these portraits were painted by personal friends of the writers, like Benjamin Robert Haydon, William Hazlitt and Joseph Severn. They have the quality of tender souvenirs, powerfully suggesting the intense solitary inner life of their sitters. For the painters, the problem of rendering this inward quality of genius, the workings of the imagination as an interior force (no longer represented by external Muses) had become the paramount artistic demand as the new touchstone of Romantic inspiration.

Several painters, like Hilton, Severn and Curran, unsatisfied with their first attempts, returned to their canvasses after the sitter's death. Their portraiture thus takes on a biographical and memorial quality, the immediate 'likeness' becoming subtly overlaid with retrospective feelings of tragic loss, of 'intimations of mortality', and the haunting sense of historical grandeur not fully recognised in the sitter's own lifetime.

The poets had, in effect, changed the painters' idea of what the genre of portraiture was really about, and why it was artistically important. The previous age had been dominated by Sir Joshua Reynolds (1723–92) and his refined concepts of classical art, dependent on Italian Renaissance models. The portrait was regarded as a highly commercial form, valuable

JOSEPH SEVERN
Self-portrait, *c.*1820

JOHN KEATS
Joseph Severn, 1819

as a source of commissions (Reynolds was receiving 50 guineas for a head and 200 guineas for a full-length portrait by the end of his career), and for social advancement, an entrée into the houses of the aristocracy. Reynolds competed fiercely with Romney and Gainsborough for this market, and produced what are now regarded as characteristic masterpieces of the period, including pictures of Dr Johnson, David Garrick and Oliver Goldsmith. Yet in the aesthetic hierarchy of art, as defined in Reynolds's Fifteen Discourses to the Royal Academy, portraiture was still assigned a lowly status similar to still-life painting or landscape, and rarely rose above 'correct and just imitation' unless combined with a grand historical subject (*Discourse III*, December 1770). The great ambition of the early Romantic generation – especially Northcote, Fuseli, West and Haydon – remained the painting of large historical canvasses: battles, Biblical scenes, Shakespearian incidents or classical myths. These were peopled by gods and goddesses, kings and heroes; not living men and women.

The emergence of Romantic portraiture was therefore almost an accident. The painters came to realise that a great historical event – Romanticism – actually surrounded them, and as Shelley claimed it was the 'poets who were the unacknowledged legislators of the world'. The gods and heroes were alive in the next room; sometimes in the same room. The new artistic challenge became evident: how to render the force of individual personality, the workings of creative genius, the inner springs of creation, in the direct realistic account of a human face? How could a satisfactory human 'likeness' somehow be given the divine and heroic spark?

By some artists, this was even regarded as a scientific problem. The study of phrenology provided a theoretical basis for reading the human features, and especially the shape of the skull, as a direct physical expression of character traits, inner powers and dominant emotions. It was first popularised in Paris in 1807 through the lectures of the Viennese physician Franz Joseph Gall. He argued that not merely general temperament, but also specific faculties like Memory and Imagination, produced recognisable formations of the cranium, brow and facial features. The widespread use of both life-masks and death-masks (the former often extremely painful to execute) was prompted by this pseudo-science. Yet it did have successes of another, unexpected kind. There are few death-masks more moving than that of Keats.

There is probably no life-mask more stunningly expressive of inner power than James Deville's mask of Blake (1823), later cast in bronze. It was deliberately made to demonstrate phrenological principles, as 'representative of the Imaginative Faculty'.

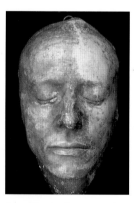

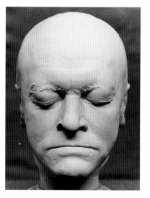

JOHN KEATS, plaster cast of death-mask by an unknown artist, 1821

WILLIAM BLAKE, Plaster life-mask made in 1953 by James S. Deville, 1823

BENJAMIN ROBERT HAYDON
Self-portrait, c.1845

JAMES NORTHCOTE
Self-portrait, 1784

But in reality there was no scientific short-cut for the painter, and everything depended on a new, psychological penetration of character and the artistic rendering of interiority. One of the most successful was James Northcote RA (1746–1831), who painted plain but noble studio portraits of Godwin and Coleridge, and numerous self-portraits. Significantly he posed himself with paint brushes in one hand, and the other pointing pensively to his own brow, to indicate the inward source of all artistic power.

Benjamin Robert Haydon (1786–1846) spent years labouring on his enormous and unfinished canvas of *Christ's Entry into Jerusalem*, but came to realise that the most valuable things in it were the faces of his friends Wordsworth, Hazlitt and Keats that he had casually slipped into the crowd. His true historical masterpiece was a portrait of Wordsworth in old age (1842), set upon the stormy evening mountainside of Helvellyn, in a pose of almost monumental inward thought. Highly introspective himself, Haydon kept a remarkable Journal, which he completed on the day he committed suicide.

Thomas Phillips RA (1770–1845) based much of his career on literary portraiture, producing notable studies of Blake, Byron, Coleridge and Davy. He was particularly admired for the 'noble gloom' with which he revealed the Romantic intensity of his sitters. In 1818 he was commissioned by John Murray to produce a whole gallery of portraits of leading authors to decorate the publisher's office in Albemarle Street, London. This Romantic Pantheon, unique of its kind, included Scott, Byron, Coleridge, Southey, Campbell and Rogers, several of whom hang there to this day.

But many of the most successful Romantic portraits were private, unpaid for, acts of friendship or passionate homage. It was as if the touch of personal intimacy alone could yield up the secrets of a writer's inner world. The American painter Washington Allston (1779–1843), when trying to capture the fluctuating genius of his friend Coleridge in middle-age (1814) remarked on the supreme difficulty of rendering this essential, inward, fleeting quality of the poet's mysterious power: 'So far as I can judge the likeness is a true one. But it is Coleridge in repose, and though not unstirred by the perpetual groundswell of his everworking intellect … it is not Coleridge in his highest mood – the poetic state. When in that state no face I ever saw was like his, it seemed almost spirit made visible, without a shadow of the physical upon it. But it was beyond the reach of my art.' (*Life and Letters*, 1893) Many of the poets had similar reservations about their own images; but they could be devastatingly funny on the subject, as will be found in this collection.

Nonetheless the achievement of Romantic portraiture in Britain did make something of what Hazlitt called 'the Spirit of the Age' both visible and supremely memorable. It encompassed not merely the poets who have become almost the symbols of creativity itself, but also the entire intellectual panorama of that great period of turmoil and aspiration. The anarchist philosopher William Godwin, the great experimental scientist Sir Humphry Davy, the critic and dream-haunted English Opium Eater Thomas De Quincey, the gothic novelist Mary Shelley, the impassioned feminist Mary Wollstonecraft – all are present with a force of individual life and imaginative energy which calls us back to one of the greatest periods of British art and culture.

Lord Byron would certainly have scoffed at the idea of canonisation, as an incurable vulgarity. Yet these Romantic figures have gradually become our icons of genius, the secular saints of our national heritage. They stare out at us, they gaze back into our own hearts, they silently challenge us to match them in their daring and their intensity.

Select Bibliography

Frances Blanshard, *Portraits of Wordsworth*, London, 1959.

T.S.R. Boase, *The Oxford History of English Art*, Oxford, 1950.

Anthony Burton and John Murdoch, *Byron*, exhibition catalogue, Victoria and Albert Museum, London,1974.

William Gilpin, *Three Essays: On Picturesque Beauty; On Picturesque Travel; On Sketching Landscape, London,* 1792.

Benjamin Robert Haydon, *Autobiography and Journals*, London, 1853.

William Hazlitt, *The Spirit of the Age*, London, 1825.

William Hazlitt, *Conversations of James Northcote*, London, 1827.

William Hazlitt, *Essays on the Fine Arts*, London, 1873.

Geoffrey Keynes, *The Complete Portraiture of William and Catherine Blake*, London, 1977.

John Opie, *Lectures On Painting* (with a Memoir by Amelia Opie), London, 1809.

Richard Ormond, *Early Victorian Portraits*, 2 vols, London, 1973.

David Parson, *Portraits of Keats*, New York, 1954.

Richard Payne Knight, *An Analytical Enquiry Into the Principles of Taste*, London, 1805.

David Piper, *The Image of the Poet: British Poets and their Portraits*, Oxford, 1982.

Sir Joshua Reynolds, *Discourses on Art*, ed. R.R. Wark, New Haven and London, 1975 (first edition 1790).

Desmond Shawe-Taylor, *Genial Company: the Theme of Genius in Eighteenth-Century British Portraiture*, exhibition catalogue, Nottingham University Art Gallery and Scottish National Portrait Gallery, 1987.

Roy Strong, *The English Icon: Elizabethan and Jacobean Portraiture*, London, 1969.

Richard Walker, *Regency Portraits*, 2 vols, London, 1985.

Ellis K. Waterhouse, *Reynolds*, London, 1941.

Richard Wendorf, *The Elements of Life: Biography and Portraiture in Stuart and Georgian England*, Oxford, 1990.

Richard Wendorf, *Sir Joshua Reynolds: the Painter in Society*, London,1996.

W.K. Wimsatt, *The Portraits of Alexander Pope*, New Haven and London, 1965.

Jonathan Wordsworth and Stephen Hebron, *Romantic Women Writers*, exhibition catalogue, The Wordsworth Trust, Dove Cottage, Grasmere, 1994.

The Unknown Romantics

❧

In 1796 the Bristol bookseller Joseph Cottle began commissioning pencil drawings of a number of unknown young poets whose work he thought might have a future. Over the next two years he published four of them with engravings of their portraits by Robert Hancock as the frontispieces to their books.

Cottle's selection was astonishingly prescient. All four of his poets were in their twenties, without literary recognition of any kind, and with undistinguished backgrounds and very chequered early careers. Yet these curiously stiff and vulnerable little profiles, which seem almost like naive photo-booth images, can be seen now as their passport pictures to future fame.

William Wordsworth (1770–1850) was from Cumberland, and after graduating from Cambridge, had lived for some time in revolutionary France where he had fathered an illegitimate child by his lover Annette Vallon.

Samuel Taylor Coleridge (1772–1834) was from Devon, had left Cambridge without a degree, and, under the pseudonym Silas Tomkyn Comberbache, temporarily joined the 15th Light Dragoons from which he was discharged as 'insane'.

WILLIAM WORDSWORTH
Robert Hancock, 1798

SAMUEL TAYLOR COLERIDGE
Robert Hancock, 1796

ROBERT SOUTHEY
Robert Hancock, 1796

CHARLES LAMB
Robert Hancock, 1798

Robert Southey (1774–1843) was from Bristol, had graduated from Oxford, and was planning to establish a utopian community in America ('Pantisocracy') and to lecture with Coleridge on revolutionary politics.

Charles Lamb (1775–1834) was born in London, had attended Christ's Hospital School with Coleridge, and after his sister Mary had gone briefly but spectacularly mad (she murdered their mother), had joined the East India Company as an office clerk.

Their early collaborative works included a verse-play *The Fall of Robespierre* (1794, Southey and Coleridge); a selection of early *Poems* (1797, Coleridge and Lamb); and the first great collection of the English Romantic movement, *Lyrical Ballads* (1798, Wordsworth and Coleridge).

The *Lyrical Ballads* astonished the reading public with its directness of style and challenging subject-matter in such poems as 'The Ancient Mariner', 'The Mad Mother', 'The Idiot Boy', 'The Thorn' and 'Tintern Abbey'. The first Romantic Circle had been formed.

WILLIAM BLAKE (1757–1827)

❧

Poet, painter and engraver, William Blake grew up in London 'conversing with angels' and retained a visionary view of the world throughout his long, hard-working and poverty-stricken career. His *Songs of Innocence and of Experience* (1794) – which contained such lyric masterpieces as 'The Sick Rose', 'The Tyger', and 'London' – sold fewer than thirty copies in his lifetime.

Powerfully influenced by the revolutions in America and France, and an idiosyncratic form of Swedenborgian mysticism, he created a series of illuminated 'prophetic books' including *Visions of the Daughters of Albion* (1793), *The Four Zoas* (1804), *Milton* (1808), and *Jerusalem* (1820). Well-known in the radical circle of Mary Wollstonecraft, Tom Paine and William Godwin, he retained a fierce, eccentric independence and was arrested on a charge of treason at Chichester in 1803, though found not-guilty. His antinomian views are memorably expressed in 'The Proverbs of Hell' (1790) with aphoristic force: 'The tigers of wrath are wiser than the horses of instruction.'

Blake's marriage to the beautiful Catherine Boucher, daughter of a London market-gardener, with whom he sunbathed naked in his garden at Lambeth, was childless but intensely happy. Towards the end of his life his poetry was recognised by Coleridge, Wordsworth and Southey, and he was extensively interviewed on his beliefs by the journalist Henry Crabb Robinson. He attracted a circle of young followers, including the painters John Linnell and Samuel Palmer, who called themselves 'The Ancients' in his honour. He died singing at Fountain Court, off the Strand. His beautiful poem from *Milton*, known as 'Jerusalem', has become adopted as the 'alternative' British national anthem: 'And did those feet in ancient time/ Walk upon England's mountains green?'

His disciple Frederick Tatham described Blake as short, stocky and energetic, with strange prominent blue eyes, and a habit of constantly rolling a pencil, paint brush or engraver's burin between his fingers. 'My fingers Emit sparks of fire with Expectation of my future labours,' wrote Blake. 'I have very little of Mr Blake's company,' said Catherine once, 'he is always in Paradise.'

Thomas Phillips's portrait was commissioned by the publisher R.H. Cromek, and shows Blake sitting uneasily in the corner of a mahogany bench, uncharacteristically wearing a smart white waistcoat and cravat, and a gold seal on a red ribbon, the outfit of a successful small-businessman. The tense position, upward glance, and poised right hand holding a pencil, suggest Blake's mind is on higher things and he is impatient to get back to work. Phillips later recalled that during the sitting Blake described a vision of the Archangel Gabriel ascending though his studio ceiling.

The bronze head illustrated here was cast from the plaster life-mask executed by the sculptor and phrenologist James Deville in 1823 to illustrate the 'Faculty of Imagination'. The cannon-ball skull and closed eyes vividly suggest the power and inwardness of Blake's visions.

A disturbing hint of the gargoyle animates John Linnell's penetrating study of Blake in old age. The drawing is based on one of Linnell's own ivory miniatures (1821; Fitzwilliam Museum, Cambridge), and was copied by the artist in 1861 for Gilchrist's biography (1863). For this later version Linnell allowed himself a freer retrospective interpretation of Blake's visionary power.

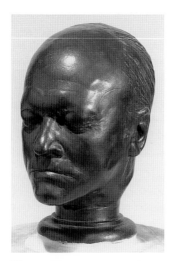

WILLIAM BLAKE, Bronze cast of
life-mask by James S. Deville, 1823

WILLIAM BLAKE
John Linnell, 1861

MARY WOLLSTONECRAFT (1759–97)

The founder of the British feminist movement, Mary Wollstonecraft was also the author of travel books, short stories, novels and influential works on children's education. Half-Irish by birth, tempestuous and articulate by nature, she started a school in Newington Green with her great friend Fanny Blood, travelled in Portugal, and settled in London in 1787, working as a journalist and translator for the radical publisher Joseph Johnson. There she met Tom Paine, William Blake and William Godwin, and in 1792 published *A Vindication of the Rights of Woman*.

She lived in Paris during the French Revolution, and had a child by the American Gilbert Imlay. In 1795 she travelled in Scandinavia, published *A Short Residence in Sweden, Norway and Denmark* and, abandoned by Imlay, tried to commit suicide by throwing herself into the River Thames. She fell in love with Godwin, conceived a second daughter – the future Mary Shelley – but died in childbirth at the age of thirty-eight. Godwin wrote her biography in 1798, which caused great scandal, and Shelley put her into his revolutionary poem *The Revolt of Islam* (1817).

Handsome and dashing, with an unruly mass of auburn hair, she was frequently painted by her contemporaries. The novelist Amelia Alderson, who had been her rival in love for William Godwin, once remarked: 'Everything I ever saw for the first time always disappointed me, except for Mary Wollstonecraft and the Cumberland Lakes.'

In his biography Godwin gave his impression of Mary Wollstonecraft in love:

> Her whole character seemed to change with her change of fortune. Her
> sorrows, the depression of spirits, were forgotten, and she assumed all the
> simplicity and vivacity of a youthful mind ... She was playful, full of
> confidence, kindness and sympathy. Her eyes assumed new lustre, and her
> cheeks new colour and smoothness. Her voice became cheerful; her temper
> overflowing with universal kindness; and that smile of bewitching
> tenderness from day to day illuminated her countenance, which all who
> knew her will so well recollect.

(Memoir, 1798)

MARY WOLLSTONECRAFT, John Opie, *c.*1797

John Opie's portrait (*c.*1797) was painted in London, when Mary Wollstonecraft was pregnant with her second child, and Godwin kept the picture above the desk in his study for the rest of his life.

WILLIAM GODWIN (1756–1836)

Political philosopher and popular novelist, William Godwin's concepts of social justice, equality, and fearless self-expression had a profound effect on many of the Romantics in their idealistic youth, including Coleridge, Wordsworth, Hazlitt and Shelley. Born in the misty fenlands of East Anglia, Godwin was educated at Hoxton Academy, London, in preparation for the Dissenting ministry, but his wide reading in the French *philosophes* such as Voltaire and Condorcet converted him to atheistic and anarchist views tending towards revolutionary Jacobinism.

Godwin's great work, *An Enquiry Concerning Political Justice* (1793), proposed republican and communitarian ideas, and attacked many institutions such as private property, marriage, and the established church, and became notorious for its defence of 'free love'. He defended a number of leading working-class radicals, including John Thelwall, in the famous Treason Trials of 1794. 'Wherever liberty, truth, justice was the theme, his name was not far off.' (Hazlitt)

A shy, modest and intensely intellectual man, he was transformed by his marriage to Mary Wollstonecraft and devastated by her early death in childbirth. Their daughter Mary subsequently ran away with his most devoted young disciple Shelley. In later life he was harried by debts and the organising capacities of his second wife Mrs Clairmont. He ran a bookshop from his house in Skinner Street, Holborn, and tried to make a living from a series of thriller novels, including *Caleb Williams* (1794), *Fleetwood* (1805), and *Mandeville* (1817).

Godwin's face – 'fine, with an expression of placid temper and recondite thought' (Hazlitt) – with its high intellectual forehead usually surmounted by a twinkling pair of round gold spectacles, entirely belied his reputation as a political firebrand. Shelley's first wife Harriet described Godwin after she had seen him in his study in 1812, shortly before Shelley had the fatal meeting with his daughter: 'His manners are so soft and pleasing that I defy even an enemy to be displeased with him … Have you ever seen a bust of Socrates, for his head is very much like that?' Even so, Godwin's name always remained associated with a Romantic idea of social progress. 'Truth is omnipotent … Man is perfectible, or in other words susceptible of perpetual improvement.' (*Political Justice*)

WILLIAM GODWIN, James Northcote, 1802

In 1825 Hazlitt observed how Godwin had mellowed:

In private, the author of Political Justice, at one time reminded those who knew him of the Metaphysician grafted on the Dissenting Minister. There was a dictatorial, captious, quibbling pettiness of manner. He lost this with the first blush and awkwardness of popularity ... He is, at present, as easy as an old glove ... There is a very admirable likeness of him by Mr Northcote.

(The Spirit of the Age, 1825)

WILLIAM WORDSWORTH (1770–1850)

The greatest poet of his age, who can be properly compared to Shakespeare and Milton for his noble conception of mankind in nature, William Wordsworth dedicated his whole life to poetry and only came slowly into his powers. His two major poems were largely composed in his thirties and forties: his verse autobiography, *The Prelude* (1805, revised 1850), and his philosophic epic, *The Excursion* (1814). He was the son of a Cumberland attorney, born at Cockermouth and educated at Hawkshead Grammar School in the Lake District. After Cambridge, Wordsworth travelled and lived in France, where he witnessed the early stages of the Revolution.

Wordsworth settled near Coleridge at Alfoxden in the Quantock Hills and together they published *Lyrical Ballads* (1798). After a period in Germany, Wordsworth finally returned to Grasmere in 1799, where he remained until his death. His passionate friendship with his younger sister Dorothy, whose famous *Journal* (1798–1803) describes their life together at Alfoxden and Grasmere in exquisite natural detail, shaped and sustained his entire career. (Ironically, Dorothy avoided having her own portrait painted, and only a paper silhouette is known.)

The shorter lyrics published in *Poems in Two Volumes* (1807), including the mysterious 'Lucy' poems, 'Daffodils', and his 'Ode: On the Intimations of Immortality from Recollections of Early Childhood', slowly established his reputation among a generation of younger admirers (such as Thomas De Quincey). Happy in his marriage and increasingly conservative in his views, he was appointed Stamp Distributor for Westmorland in 1813, wrote a *Guide to the Lakes* in 1822, and was made Poet Laureate in 1843.

Tall, taciturn, weatherbeaten, with a deep Cumberland voice and commanding presence, he impressed everyone he met with a sense of inner power. His appearance in 1798 was described by Hazlitt as 'gaunt and Don Quixote-like', with eccentric touches:

> He was quaintly dressed (accordingly to the costume of that unconstrained period) in a brown fustian jacket and striped pantaloons. There was something of a roll, a lounge in his gait, not unlike his own Peter Bell. There was a severe, worn pressure of thought about his temples, a fire in his eye (as if he saw something in objects more than the outward appearance), an intense

high narrow forehead, a Roman nose, cheeks furrowed by strong purpose and feeling, and a convulsive inclination to laughter about the mouth, a good deal at variance with the solemn, stately expression of the rest of the face.

(On My First Acquaintance with Poets, 1821)

WILLIAM WORDSWORTH
Benjamin Robert Haydon, 1818

The painter Haydon was fascinated by him, and executed the chalk drawing in 1818 as a gift for Wordsworth's wife Mary. 'He sat like a Poet and Philosopher, calm, quiet, amiable. I succeeded in a capital likeness of him.' Wordsworth later called this drawing 'The Brigand'. Wordsworth remained an active fell-walker into old age, and climbed Helvellyn to celebrate his seventieth birthday. Haydon marked this feat with the full-length picture illustrated opposite, actually executed from sittings in his London studio, but with the symbolic setting of Helvellyn at sunset painted in afterwards from memory. With its intense, brooding inwardness it is one of the great successes of Romantic portraiture.

WILLIAM WORDSWORTH, Benjamin Robert Haydon, 1842

SAMUEL TAYLOR COLERIDGE (1772–1834)

'Poet and philosopher-in a-mist' (according to his own description), fell-walker, lecturer and opium addict, Coleridge is the great inspirational figure of English Romanticism. Wordsworth called him 'the only wonderful man I ever knew'. Born at Ottery St Mary, Devon, the son of a clergyman, he attended Cambridge University, volunteered for the Dragoons, collaborated with Wordsworth on the *Lyrical Ballads* (1798), studied in Germany, and settled for four years at Keswick in the Lake District. This period saw the writing of his most famous poems, 'Kubla Khan', *The Ancient Mariner, Christabel*, 'Frost at Midnight', and 'Dejection: an Ode'.

Thereafter, his marriage broken by a disastrous love-affair (see the 'Asra' poems) and health wrecked by opium, he travelled restlessly in the Mediterranean, lectured on poetry in London and Bristol, and in 1816 finally settled at Highgate in the care of the surgeon James Gillman, where he wrote his *Aids to Reflection*, and many late poems such as 'Limbo' and 'Alice Du Clos'. His *Biographia Literaria* (1817), his collected essays in *The Friend* (1818) and his superb *Notebooks* (1794–1834) all give a vivid impression of his troubled genius.

Coleridge was a marvellous talker and autobiographer, as shown in his self-mocking description in a letter written shortly after the Vandyke portrait was painted for his publisher Cottle in 1795. This was not so much modesty, as a Romantic sense of his own peculiarities, in which chaotic inner energy was bodied forth as weakness and eccentricity:

> *My face, unless when animated by immediate eloquence, expresses great Sloth, & great, indeed almost idiotic good-nature. 'Tis a mere carcass of a face, fat flabby and expressive chiefly of inexpression. My gait is awkward, & the walk, & the Whole man indicates indolence capable of energies ... I have read almost everything – a library-cormorant – I am deep in all out of the way books.... Metaphysics, & Poetry, & 'Facts of Mind' ... I cannot breathe thro' my nose – so my mouth, with sensual thick lips, is almost always open. In conversation I am impassioned ...*

(Letter to John Thelwall, 1796)

The American painter Washington Allston had first met Coleridge in Italy, where they became lifelong friends, and his portrait of 1814 (done

SAMUEL TAYLOR COLERIDGE
Washington Allston, 1814

in Bristol when Coleridge was forty-two) presents a large, powerful, suffering man who seems immobilised in his own dreamy meditations. The plump, round silver face above the severe, black clerical garb curiously suggests the full moon on a dark night, one of Coleridge's enduring images from *The Ancient Mariner*. Coleridge wrote: 'Whatever is impressive is part fugitive, part existent only in the imaginations of persons impressed strongly with my conversation. The face itself is a FEEBLE, unmanly face ...' (*Letters*, 1814) Allston's own perceptive comments are given in the Introduction.

ROBERT SOUTHEY (1774–1843)

History has not been kind to Southey, choosing to forget almost everything he wrote except the famous children's story of *The Three Bears*. Widely admired in his lifetime as a prolific poet, essayist and historian, he was appointed Poet Laureate in 1813, and for thirty years was the most feared and influential critic on the Tory *Quarterly Review*.

Born in Bristol (a lonely child looked after by a rich and eccentric aunt), Southey was educated at Oxford, dreamed of Pantisocracy with Coleridge and wrote revolutionary verse-dramas such as *Wat Tyler* (1794, published 1817), *The Fall of Robespierre* (1794), and *Joan of Arc* (1796), which came back to haunt him in respectable middle age. He spent a formative year in Lisbon, learned Spanish and Portuguese, and returned to marry and settle at Keswick (1803) where he established a huge private library and heroically supported his own and Coleridge's large extended family with regular journalism, translation and reviewing, written to a ferocious daily timetable, with a silver pocket-watch on his desk. In Edward Nash's drawing of 1820 the metamorphosis is complete: revolutionary bard into *Quarterly* reviewer.

The exotic and splendidly titled verse-epics, over which he slaved with such devotion – *Thalaba the Destroyer* (1801), *The Curse of Kehama* (1810), *Roderick: The Last of the Goths* (1814) – were ridiculed by the younger generation. He also had the misfortune to attack both Byron and Shelley in print for their bad poetry and worse morals. Southey retreated into vast histories of Brazil and the Peninsular War, while his sister-in-law hanged herself, and his wife eventually went mad. His best writing is biographical – in remarkably assured Lives of Nelson (1813), the preacher John

ROBERT SOUTHEY, Edward Nash, 1820

Wesley (1820), and the melancholy poet Cowper (1837) – and in shrewd, funny and refreshingly outspoken letters about his famous friends, especially Lamb, Coleridge, Wordsworth, De Quincey and Walter Scott.

Southey's fine, equine, almost arrogantly handsome face was set on a gangling, long-legged body, giving him something of the appearance of a highly strung, thoroughbred racehorse. Hazlitt recalled him in his youth, before political disillusion and domesticity had curbed him:

> *Mr Southey, as we formerly remember to have seen him, had a hectic flush upon his cheek, a roving fire in his eye, a falcon glance, a look at once aspiring and dejected ... He wooed Liberty as a youthful lover, but it was perhaps more as a mistress than a bride; and he has since wedded with an elderly and not very reputable lady, called Legitimacy.*

(The Spirit of the Age, 1825)

ROBERT SOUTHEY
Henry Edridge, 1804

Many painters called to take his likeness at Keswick, especially after the Laureateship, but Southey disliked most of the results, describing one portrait by Thomas Phillips as giving his eyes 'an expression which I conceive to be more like two oysters in love than anything else'. The drawing by Henry Edridge done in Southey's study in 1804, with Derwentwater and the fells projected like a picturesque backcloth, catches better than most the domesticated bard, well-brushed and buttoned-up, clever and a touch sarcastic, with elegant socks and shoes that never tramped a hillside. Thomas Carlyle remembered him, 'all legs; in shape and stature like a pair of tongs.' (*Reminiscences*)

ROBERT SOUTHEY, Peter Vandyke, 1795

AMELIA OPIE (1769–1853)

Poet and novelist, Amelia Opie (née Alderson) was one of the great beauties of the Romantic generation, who entranced the Godwin circle with her youthful high spirits and revolutionary ardour. The clever daughter of a leading Norwich doctor, well-read in French and musically talented, she published her early poems in local papers and sang her own ballads at private receptions.

In 1794 she came to London and attended the Treason Trials of John Thelwall, Horne Tooke and Thomas Holcroft at the Old Bailey. When Horne Tooke was acquitted, she is said to have walked across the top of the barristers' table to kiss him. She was courted by Holcroft, and then Godwin, much to Mary Wollstonecraft's annoyance, but finally married the painter John Opie (recently divorced) in 1798. They visited Paris in 1802, after the publication of her *Poems* which ran to six editions. In 1804 she published her most famous work, *Adeline Mowbray, or The Mother and the Daughter*, a novel about contemporary marriage, partly based on the lives of Godwin and Mary Wollstonecraft.

After John Opie's early death in 1807, she returned to Norwich to keep house for her beloved father, and became a Quaker, dedicating her life to visiting prisons, hospitals and workhouses. In 1818, however, she said she was still writing for eight hours a day, and lamented: 'Shall I ever cease to enjoy the pleasures of this world? I fear not.' Other novels included *Father and Daughter* (1801), *Madeline* (1822), and the unfinished *The Painter and His Wife*. She kept up a wide circle of friends in both London and Paris, including Byron, Scott, Wordsworth, Madame de Staël and Lafayette. In 1814 she was reported as 'dancing vivaciously in a pink domino at the ball given to the Duke of Wellington in Devonshire House'. (*DNB*) When she died a street was named after her in Norwich.

With her large brown eyes, clear bold features and voluptuous figure (which became good-naturedly plump in middle-age) Mrs Opie always attracted clever men and alarmed clever women. Crabb Robinson noted that 'her becoming a Quakeress gave her a sort of éclat' (*Diary*, 1824); Mrs Inchbald called her 'cleverer than her books'; while Miss Sedgwick cattily observed that her 'elaborate simplicity and the fashionable little train to her pretty satin gown indicated how much easier it is to adopt a theory than to change one's habits.' (*Letters from Abroad*) John Opie's portrait is

AMELIA OPIE, John Opie, 1798

a tender tribute to his wife, painted in the year of their marriage. Its intimacy is emphasised by the direct unflinching gaze (with its hint of mischief), the fullness of the mouth, and the casual placing of the formal hat with its riding veil on her knee. The beautifully braided hair subtly suggests a laurel wreath, symbol of literary renown.

Charles Lamb (1775–1834)

The most kind and lovable of men, Lamb set out to be a poet but found his true identity as an essayist and whimsical autobiographer. He created the persona of 'Elia' who could enliven any subject under the sun, from reading Shakespeare to eating roast pig for supper. The son of a lawyer's clerk of the Inner Temple, Lamb attended Christ's Hospital School with Coleridge, and then worked for forty years as a clerk in the East India Company in the City.

Almost all Lamb's work is a celebration of London and the metropolitan sensibility, just as his closest friends celebrated the Lake District and wild nature. One of his most penetrating early essays was *On the Genius and*

CHARLES LAMB, William Hazlitt, 1804

Character of Hogarth (1811). His occasional poems, tender and elegiac, include 'The Old Familiar Faces' (1798), the ballad 'Hester' (1803), and the infinitely touching 'On an Infant Dying as Soon as Born' (1827).

Insanity dogged Lamb's family: Lamb himself spent six weeks in Hoxton Lunatic Asylum in 1795, and the following year his beloved elder sister Mary was incarcerated there for five months after fatally stabbing their mother during a paranoid episode. Lamb dedicated the rest of his life to looking after Mary, and together they published *Tales from Shakespeare* (1807) and *Adventures of Ulysses* (1808) for children. His rooms near the Strand became the late-night meeting place for his many friends including Coleridge, Wordsworth, Southey, Hazlitt, Haydon, and Leigh Hunt. Here Lamb presided in a celestial cloud of tobacco smoke, port fumes and precipitate puns, brought to earth with his inimitable stutter. The first collected volume of the *Essays of Elia*, dedicated to Coleridge, appeared in 1823; and the second in 1833. When he died Wordsworth mourned him in a poem as 'Lamb, the frolic and the gentle'.

Small, animated, deeply eccentric and often rather drunk, no painter ever captured Lamb's pixie-like and mischievous charm. He had one brown eye and one grey. His reply to Coleridge's loving epithet, 'my gentle-hearted Charles' (in the poem 'This Lime-Tree Bower My Prison'), was characteristic: 'call me rather drunken-dog, ragged head, seldom-shaven, odd-ey'd, stuttering, or any other epithet which truly and properly belongs.' (*Letters*, 1797) He got his own back twenty years later by calling Coleridge, in a superb phrase, 'an Archangel a little Damaged'. (*Letters*, 1816) Leigh Hunt wrote: 'Charles Lamb had a head worthy of Aristotle, with as fine a heart as ever beat in a human bosom, and limbs very fragile to sustain it ... There never was a true portrait of Lamb.' (*Autobiography*, 1850)

The best attempt is Hazlitt's curiously solemn picture of 1804, one of the last he ever painted before taking up writing, which Crabb Robinson dryly described as 'certainly the only painting by Hazlitt that I ever saw with pleasure'. (*Diary*, 1812) The seventeenth-century Spanish costume was not the result of Lamb dressing-up (like Byron in Albanian draperies) for theatrical effect as an Iberian Elia. It was instead a typical act of lambent friendship: Hazlitt wanted to do a copy of Velazquez's *Philip IV*, and Lamb had humbly agreed to act as his clothes-horse. One can only imagine the philippic puns that accompanied the sitting.

William Hazlitt (1778–1830)
❦

Political journalist and superb all-round critic of the arts (from poetry to pugilism), Hazlitt became the radical conscience of Romanticism. Famed equally for the gusto of his prose and the bitterness of his quarrels, he was a lifelong republican. The son of a Unitarian preacher from Wiltshire, Hazlitt first trained for the Dissenting ministry, and then as a portrait-painter, but inspired by a meeting with Coleridge and Wordsworth in the Quantocks in 1798, he gradually took up freelance writing. This experience is memorably described in one of his greatest essays: *On My First Acquaintance with Poets* (1821).

Hazlitt could write with equal brilliance on theatre, painting, boxing, politics, poetry or long-distance walking. Keats said that 'the depth of Hazlitt's taste' was one of the three glories of the age (the other two being Wordsworth's poetry and Haydon's pictures). His major essays were collected in *The Characters of Shakespeare's Plays* (1817), *Political Essays* (1819), *Lectures on The English Comic Writers* (1819) and *Winterslow* (1831, named after his writing retreat on the edge of Salisbury Plain). He produced a vivid and often devastating assessment of his contemporaries in a gallery of twenty-five pen portraits (including Coleridge, Wordsworth, Southey, Godwin, Byron and Scott) collected as *The Spirit of the Age* (1825).

Lonely and mercurial, he was twice married (both times unhappily), and in 1823 published *Liber Amoris*, the agonised account of his unrequited passion for Sarah Walker, a sixteen-year-old servant-girl. His conversations with the painter James Northcote, an interesting experiment in biography, were collected as *Boswell Redivivus* (1827). Hazlitt ended his days in tragic isolation and poverty, working on an unfinished Life of his hero Napoleon, and sending a last letter to the editor of the *Edinburgh Review* from his Soho lodgings: 'Dear Sir, I am dying; can you send me £10, and so consummate your many kindnesses to me?' (*Letters*, 1830)

Hazlitt's extraordinary mixture of shyness and aggression was not easily captured on canvas. The Bewick sketch was done during his second honeymoon at Melrose in Scotland, and his wife remarked 'Oh, it is exactly your own hair, my dear.' (T. Landseer, *Life of Bewick*, 1871) His friend George Patmore recalled him as 'a pale anatomy of a man ... the forehead was magnificent, the nose strong, light and elegant, the mouth greatly resembled Edmund Kean's, the eyes grey (furtive), sometimes sinister,

WILLIAM HAZLITT, William Bewick, 1825

never brilliant, the head nobly formed with a profusion of coal-black curls.' (*My Friends and Acquaintances*, 1854)

Coleridge, whom Hazlitt both praised and mocked, got as close as anyone with this memorable verbal portrait of Hazlitt at twenty-four:

> *William Hazlitt is a thinking, observant, original man ... His manners are to 99 in 100 singularly repulsive – brow-hanging, shoe-contemplative, strange ... he is, I verily believe, kindly-natured ... but he is jealous, gloomy, & of an irritable Pride – & addicted to women, as objects of sexual Indulgence. With all this there is much good in him ... he says things that are his own in a way of his own ... he sends well-headed & well-feathered Thoughts straight forwards to the mark with a Twang of the Bow-string.'*
>
> (Letters, 1802)

MARY ROBINSON (1758–1800)

Poet, actress, novelist and adventuress, Mary 'Perdita' Robinson was one of the most glamorous and talented women of her generation who embodied the early spirit of Romanticism in her life as much as her work. She played many of Shakespeare's heroines in the London theatres

MARY ROBINSON, George Dance, *c.*1793

between 1778 and 1790, and in the last decade of her career published seven novels and three volumes of poetry. She knew Godwin, and befriended the young Coleridge, hearing him recite 'Kubla Khan' sixteen years before the poem was published; and was powerfully influenced by the *Lyrical Ballads* (1798) in her later work.

Married at sixteen to a feckless husband (with whom she spent ten months in prison for debt), Mary Robinson took to the stage and caught the eye of the teenage Prince of Wales while playing Perdita in *The Winter's Tale* at Covent Garden in 1779. After a heady year as the royal mistress (from whence her nickname), she moved into the bed of the great Opposition statesman Charles James Fox who arranged for her to receive a state pension of £500 per annum (a considerable sum, giving her complete independence), and then formed a passionate but fraught alliance with a distinguished military historian and MP, the roving Colonel Tarleton, which lasted on and off till the end of her life.

In 1792 she visited revolutionary France (in the middle of a lover's quarrel). But a near-fatal miscarriage left her increasingly paralysed with an agonising form of arthritis, and in her remarkable *Memoirs* (published posthumously in 1801) she describes how she took opium against the pain, and wrote under its influence in a way very similar to Coleridge. While her novels are sentimental, her poetry has unexpected dash and clarity, very much in her own voice, sometimes racily satirical, but always stylish.

Like the other Romantics she made poetry out of the incidents of her own life, but also identified very early on the subjects that would attract her male contemporaries. Her *Poems* (1791) include an 'Ode to Melancholy', and an 'Ode to the Nightingale', as well as 'Monody to the Memory of Chatterton' and 'Sonnet: the Mariner'. In the year of her death, Coleridge wrote her a touching poem of greeting and farewell, 'A Stranger Minstrel', praising her 'witching melody'.

Famous for her imperious beauty (as well as her dramatic hats), Mary Robinson was frequently painted by Romney, Gainsborough, Reynolds and Zoffany. But for them she was primarily an actress on display. George Dance's intimate, rather melancholy drawing, done in later life (*c*.1793) shows her instead as a writer more at home in her private study, wrapped up in a plain day dress with her hair pulled back in a practical – but typically flamboyant – silk scarf with its seductive bow.

Thomas De Quincey (1785–1859)

The strangest and most exotic of the Romantics, De Quincey made his name at the age of thirty-seven with his *Confessions of an English Opium Eater* (1821), written in a garret off Covent Garden and originally published the previous year in two instalments by the *London Magazine*. Scholarly, fantastical, deeply read in German and Oriental literature, De Quincey was a gentleman bohemian who supported himself, a large family, and his lifelong drug-addiction by a huge output of journalism. He became the master of a baroque form of autobiographical dream-prose, and a critic of peculiar psychological insights. His taste for the grotesque, and his combination of arcane learning with black humour, is brilliantly displayed in his essays, *On Murder Considered as One of the Fine Arts* and *On the Knocking on the Gate in Macbeth*.

The son of a wealthy linen merchant, eccentric in his habits and diminutive in stature (he was barely five foot tall), De Quincey absconded first from Manchester Grammar School, and then from Oxford, drifting through Wales and London, reading the poetry of Wordsworth and Coleridge, taking opium, and living with a teenage prostitute whom he tenderly describes in his *Confessions* as 'Ann of Oxford Street'. In 1808 he settled in the Lake District near his idol Wordsworth, taking over Dove Cottage and filling it with fifty-six tea-chests of books.

De Quincey's memories of this time, shrewd and mischievous, later appeared as *Recollections of the Lake Poets* (1834–9) with memorable portraits of William and Dorothy Wordsworth, Coleridge and Southey. He lived with the daughter of a local farmer, whom he finally married in 1817, producing eight children. Thereafter he drifted between London and Edinburgh, writing irregular but brilliant essays in his 'impassioned prose', including an unfinished study of his opium-dreams, *Suspiria De Profundis* (1845, *Sighs from the Deep*), and the thrilling, moonlit vision of disaster entitled *The English Mail Coach* (1849). His work made an immediate impact in France, second only to Byron's, and was translated by Baudelaire in *Les Paradis Artificiels*, and praised by Gautier.

When De Quincey first came to Grasmere, Dorothy Wordsworth was entranced by his ability to play with the children, and he always retained an impish, changeling quality as if his whole life was some fantastic, labyrinthian game. 'We feel often as if he were one of the Family – he is

loving, gentle and happy – a very good scholar, and an acute Logician …
His person is unfortunately *diminutive*, but there is a sweetness in his
looks, especially about the eyes, which soon overcomes the oddness in
your first feeling at the sight of so very little a Man.' (*Letters*, 1808)

In later life, when opium and poverty had taken their toll, Crabb
Robinson observed a pale wizened creature, whose strangeness was
nonetheless still attractive: 'In London he could not possibly maintain
himself. I saw him occasionally there as a shiftless man. He had a
wretchedly invalid countenance: his skin looked like mother-of-pearl. He
had a very delicate hand & voice more soft than a woman's, but his conversation was highly intelligent and interesting.' (*Reminiscences*, 1843) Sir
John Watson-Gordon's portrait was done at about this time (*c*.1845). The
large, heavy, handsome overcoat with its furred collar and sleeves, seems
deliberately designed to disguise the shrunken, penniless, haunted Opium
Eater within.

SIR HUMPHRY DAVY (1778–1829)

The greatest British scientist of his day and President of the Royal Society, Davy was also an intimate friend of Coleridge and Wordsworth, knew Scott and Byron, and was a gifted minor poet in his own right. He published a delightful volume of piscatorial reflections (in dialogue form), *Salmonia, or Days of Fly-Fishing* (1828), and a moving book of meditations, *Consolations in Travel, or the Last Days of a Philosopher* (1830). His brilliant career shows no evidence of the modern split between the 'two cultures', and his ability to explain and popularise his experimental

SIR HUMPHRY DAVY, Thomas Phillips, 1821

work in books and lectures (which particularly influenced Coleridge) suggests that there was once such a thing as Romantic Science. He wrote: 'Whilst chemical pursuits exalt the understanding, they do not depress the imagination or weaken genuine feeling.'

A Cornishman by birth, Davy studied at the famous Bristol Pneumatic Institution under Dr Thomas Beddoes (where Coleridge joined him in experiments with laughing gas), and oversaw the proof-corrections to the *Lyrical Ballads*. In 1803 he was appointed Professor of Chemistry at the newly founded Royal Institution in London, and began his celebrated Bakerian Lectures at the Royal Society, demonstrating the electrical affinity of chemical elements and isolating sodium and potassium. Like a true Romantic he had an instinctive appreciation of fire and combustion, inventing in 1813 the famous Davy Safety Lamp, an 'insulated light' which did not ignite the lethal hydrogen or methane gases in deep-pit mine shafts. Another of his more hazardous experiments was to launch Coleridge as a lecturer at the Royal Institution in 1808.

In 1812 he was knighted for his work, and received many other honours both in London and Paris. However, his marriage of the same year to a fashionable Scottish blue-stocking, Jane Apreece, was childless and increasingly discordant. By the time he was appointed President of the Royal Society (1820), he had become an isolated and tragically embittered man, cut off from his friends, gloomy and introspective, and suffering from progressive heart-disease. His great protégé, Michael Faraday, found him cold and remote. Davy travelled much on the Continent, drinking and writing (like Coleridge and Shelley he produced a long poem on 'Mont Blanc'), and died alone in a hotel room in Geneva aged fifty. But he left the Romantics with a noble and dynamic view of the physical universe, as a constant flux of energies and mysterious forms.

An attractive, rather boyish figure, with dark Celtic features and a commanding nose, Davy burst into life on the lecture platform and had the gift of enchanting his audiences. 'He is now about thirty-three', wrote George Ticknor in 1815, 'but with all the freshness and bloom of five-and-twenty, and one of the handsomest men I have seen in England.' (*Life and Letters*, 1876) Phillips's portrait was executed after a miners' banquet in Davy's honour at Newcastle, and shows the elegant shape of the Davy Lamp that saved so many of their lives, placed proudly at his elbow.

LORD BYRON
Thomas Phillips, 1835, after the portrait of 1813

LORD BYRON (1788–1824)

With Lord Byron, English Romanticism became an international style. A charismatic figure of devastating charm and vanity, Byron became the beau ideal of the Romantic writer while pretending to do nothing so unspeakably vulgar. His poems became effortless best-sellers, his letters are among the finest and funniest in the language, and his stormy private life inspired over two hundred biographies and memoirs. His masterpiece is *Don Juan*, an autobiographical poem in five Cantos begun in 1818, which reflects his lifelong travels through Europe and the Levant, and is written in his wonderful world-weary style of mocking colloquialisms and lyric irony.

His father 'Mad Jack' Byron died when he was only three, and Byron grew up at Newstead Abbey, a dilapidated gothic pile in Nottinghamshire, a clever, lonely and passionate child who was always haunted by a secret 'mark of Cain', his club-foot. At Cambridge he formed a brilliant circle of dandyish friends (one of them, Scrope Davies, noted that he slept in paper-curlers), and in 1809 set the literary establishment on fire with his satire 'English Bards and Scotch Reviewers'.

He came back from two years' wanderings in Spain, Malta, Greece and Turkey, to publish the first two Cantos of *Childe Harold's Pilgrimage* (1812) and 'awoke to find myself famous'. These were followed by several Oriental verse-tales (*The Corsair* was written in ten days) and a glorious period of social lionising, including his scandalous affair with the volatile Lady Caroline Lamb (1785–1828), who dressed for him as a page-boy.

Lady Caroline Lamb subsequently published a gothic novel of her passionate entanglement with Byron, *Glenarvon* (1816), and died insane twelve years later.

Byron worked for the Drury Lane Theatre Committee, made lasting alliances with Walter Scott and the poet Tom Moore (a future biographer, 1830) and encouraged Coleridge to publish 'Christabel'. But the liaison with his half-sister Augusta Leigh, and the collapse of his marriage to Arabella Millbank, drove him abroad again in 1816, to settle in Italy with his menagerie of Venetian mistresses and exotic animals, brilliantly evoked in his poem *Beppo* (1818). In 1821 he moved to the Palazzo Lanfranchi, Pisa, with the Countess Teresa Guiccioli, a bulldog and a billiard-table.

His magnetic presence attracted Shelley and Mary (whose half-sister Claire Clairmont became another mistress), and innumerable raffish admirers and hangers-on. Among these were the young Scottish physician John William Polidori (1795–1821), author of *The Vampyre* (1819), and shortly after a suicide. Most striking was Edward John Trelawny (1792–1881), a bearded Cornish adventurer and inspired teller of tall stories, who cast himself as a natural Byronic hero and accompanied Byron to the Greek War of Independence in 1822. His *Records of Shelley, Byron and the Author* (1858) is a vividly convincing and totally unreliable work of Romantic biography.

JOHN WILLIAM POLIDORI
F. G. Gainsford, *c.*1816

EDWARD JOHN TRELAWNY
Joseph Severn, 1838

Byron's final commitment to the Philhellene cause in Greece electrified the youth of Europe and hundreds rushed to join him. His private disillusion in the brutal chaos of the war, witnessed in his last letters and poems ('Tis time this heart should be unmoved', dated Missolonghi, 22 January 1824), was offset by extraordinary courage and generosity, and an unflinching dedication to 'Freedom's battle'. Stylish and self-mocking to the end (he sported a plumed helmet but lamented the grey hairs beneath), his death from fever at Missolonghi in April 1824 was mourned throughout Europe and signalled the apotheosis of Romanticism. In Lincolnshire, on hearing the news, a young poet called Tennyson carved 'Byron is Dead' upon a rock.

Byron's fine, aristocratic beauty was admired equally by men and women, and inspired dozens of pictures, sketches, busts and medallions both during his lifetime and after. The large head with its dark curls, the mocking eyes and voluptuous mouth, distracted from the stocky body always tending to overweight, and the distinctive limp with its hint of the cloven hoof. He was Apollo combined with Mephistopheles.

'Lord Byron's head', wrote John Gibson Lockhart, 'is without doubt the finest in our time – I think it better on the whole, than either Napoleon's, or Goethe's, or Canova's, or Wordsworth's.' (*Letters*, 1819) Byron himself was typically droll on the matter: 'my personal charms have by no means increased – my hair is half grey – and the Crow's foot has been rather lavish of its indelible steps – my hair though not gone is going – and my teeth remain by way of courtesy – but I suppose they will follow.' (*Letters*, 1819) But Coleridge recalled that being in Byron's presence was like seeing the sun. (*Letters*, 1816)

Lord Byron
E. H. Bailey, 1826

Sir Walter Scott (1771–1832)

❧

Now remembered as our greatest historical novelist, author of over thirty volumes of the *Waverley* series, Scott first made his name as a poet and prolific writer of Romantic verse-tales. He had no reputation as a novelist until his mid-forties, and his work was seen primarily as a rival to Southey's and Byron's. Fascinated by the Border Ballads of his native lowlands, and a skilful translator of German gothic ballads by Bürger and Goethe (which also attracted Coleridge and Wordsworth), he published *Minstrelsy of the Scottish Borders* in 1802–3.

Scott popularised a form of highly musical, melodramatic, 'antiquarian' verse-tales of the Highlands – battles, hauntings, castles, lakes, and star-crossed lovers – whose titles still hold an ineffable, misty romance: *The Lay of the Last Minstrel* (1805), *The Lady of the Lake* (1810), *The Bridal of Triermain* (1813), and *The Lord of the Isles* (1815). It was only when his audience was finally captured by Byron that he turned to prose and the vast resources of Scottish clan history. Among his outstanding achievements were the original *Waverley* (1814), *Old Mortality* (1816), *Rob Roy* (1817), *The Heart of Midlothian* (1817), *Ivanhoe* (1819), *Quentin Durward* (1823), and *Castle Dangerous* (1831).

As the author of such wild and aboriginal romances, Scott's solid, genial and meticulous nature presents a curious paradox. He was educated at Edinburgh University, successfully trained for the Scottish bar, became a partner in Ballantyne's publishing house, helped found the *Quarterly Review*, and took immense pride in his manse at Abbotsford on the Tweed, which he purchased in 1811. He was Sheriff-depute of Selkirkshire, and was knighted in 1820. It was wholly characteristic of him that he refused the Poet Laureateship (in Southey's favour) in 1813; and when Ballantyne's went bankrupt in 1826, he shouldered the huge debt of £114,000 and gradually paid off his debtors from the profits of his pen – an heroic effort which undoubtedly shortened his life. The one shadow in his professional career was that he was accused, with some reason, of plagiarising Coleridge's *Christabel* in his early work; but this could be taken as a compliment.

Gruff, witty, hospitable, hard-working and hard-drinking – every inch a Scotsman – Scott was often painted in his lair at Abbotsford. 'There was more benevolence expressed in Scott's face', said his friend the painter

SIR WALTER SCOTT, Sir Edwin Landseer, *c.*1824

C.R. Leslie, 'than is given in any portrait of him.' (*Autobiographical Recollections*, 1865) But the fine, florid, distinguished features – with hair prematurely silver – and tall, powerful body, all spoke clearly of his inner strength and creative force. What was harder to capture was his primitive quality, the man who heard the auld lang' syne so clearly calling from the glens. Landseer went up to paint his portrait at Abbotsford in 1824, while Scott was working on *Redgauntlet*. 'He has painted every dog in the house', remarked Scott, 'and ended up with the owner.' (*Letters*, 1824)

PERCY BYSSHE SHELLEY (1792–1822)

As reckless and brilliant in his poetry as in his life, Shelley poured out the great body of his major work in less than a decade, and drowned (with two friends) off the coast of Tuscany at the age of twenty-nine, while trying to race a summer storm back to Lerici in his small yacht, and pressing on with full sail. He is still popularly remembered as a love poet ('Lines Written in the Bay of Lerici'), a master of plangent lyrics ('To a Skylark'), of superb odes ('To the West Wind') and moving elegies ('Adonais', on the death of Keats). But he was also a philosophical and political essayist, and a gifted poetic translator from German, Italian, Greek, Spanish and Arabic.

Many of Shelley's radical and revolutionary ideas, powerfully influenced by his father-in-law William Godwin, were expressed in his great dramatic poem *Prometheus Unbound* (1820). He wrote wonderful letters about his travels in Italy, describing it as 'the Paradise of Exiles', and an historic *Defence of Poetry* (1821). Wordsworth called him 'one of the best *artists* of us all; I mean in workmanship of style'.

The rebellious son of a Sussex baronet, Shelley was educated at Eton and Oxford (from which he was sent down for atheism), and was twice married. His first wife, Harriet Westbrook, committed suicide in the Serpentine; his second wife, Mary Godwin, wrote *Frankenstein*; and two of his children died in Italy. His complex relationship with Byron is described in one of his finest, plainest and most haunting poems, 'Julian and Maddalo' (1818). His friend Thomas Love Peacock (1785–1866) affectionately satirised him – along with Byron and Coleridge – as the unworldly idealist Scythrop Glowry in the novel *Nightmare Abbey* (1818).

At the time of his death, while living at his remote beach-house the Casa Magni in San Terenzo, Shelley was working on a long poem in *terza rima* based on Dante's *Inferno*, the visionary 'Triumph of Life'. Parts of this manuscript are written on the back of drawings of the sailing-rig for his yacht the *Ariel*.

Thin, wide-eyed, intense, Shelley was an expert pistol-shot, a good horse-rider, an athletic walker and a convinced vegetarian. Impetuous by temperament, much troubled by physical seizures (probably kidney stones) and psychic manifestations, he lived with an unsettling urgency that affected all those around him. His sensible banker friend, Horace

PERCY BYSSHE SHELLEY, Amelia Curran, 1819

THOMAS LOVE PEACOCK, Roger Jean, *c.*1805

Smith, called him 'a psychological curiosity, infinitely more curious than Coleridge's Kubla Khan'.

The only authentic portrait of Shelley was painted by Amelia Curran in her studio near the Spanish Steps in Rome; at the time he was finishing *Prometheus Unbound* in 1819. (Curran later told Mary Shelley that she had almost burned the picture, because it was 'so ill done' and had failed to capture his restless spirit.) Leigh Hunt, who saw Shelley in the port of Livorno, a few days before he drowned, left a memorable description:

> *His figure was tall and slight, and his constitution consumptive. He was subject to violent spasmodic pains ... his shoulders were bent a little, owing to premature thought and trouble ... Like the Stagyrite's, his voice was high and weak. His eyes were large and animated, with a dash of wildness in them ... He had brown hair, which, though tinged with grey, surmounted his face well, being in considerable quantity, and tending to curl ... when fronting and looking at you attentively his aspect had a certain seraphical character that would have suited a portrait of John the Baptist, or the angel whom Milton describes as holding a reed 'tipt' with fire.*

(Autobiography, 1850)

MARY SHELLEY (1797–1851)

Celebrated as the author of one unforgettable book, *Frankenstein, or The Modern Prometheus*, published when she was twenty-one, Mary Shelley was actually a professional *femme de lettres* of many talents and striking versatility. She wrote six major novels, over forty short stories, a travel book (based on her Continental adventures with Shelley), and numerous essays and short biographies. She also produced an autobiographical novella of her mental breakdown in Italy, *Mathilda* (1819), and a confessional poem about her life after Shelley's death, 'The Choice' (1822) – both unpublished until the twentieth century – as well as the moving biographical 'Notes' to the 1839 edition of Shelley's *Collected Poems*.

The beautiful only child of William Godwin and Mary Wollstonecraft (who died in childbirth), she was her father's darling and was privately educated to a standard far higher than usually achieved at Oxford, or at Cambridge (Girton, the first college for women, was not founded until 1869). After her elopement with Shelley in 1814 (which shattered Godwin as much as her mother's death had sixteen years previously), she published her first book anonymously, *History of a Six Weeks Tour* (1817), in collaboration with Shelley.

Frankenstein, also anonymous, followed in 1818, on the eve of their departure for Italy. Inspired by a ghost-story competition with Byron and Polidori at the Villa Diodati, Lake Geneva, in the summer of 1816, it broke the conventions of the eighteenth-century gothic novel to become the first recognisable work of modern science fiction. Its celebrated 'eight foot' Monster (subsequently the star of a score of modern films, of which the best by far is Kenneth Branagh's, 1994) is as much a Romantic Outcast, a sort of Adam after the Fall, as a Hammer House horror-figure with a bolt through his head. Much of Mary's own scientific reading about electrical phenomena and anatomy, as well as her own terrible experiences in childbirth, went into the book; and it has been convincingly argued that Dr Frankenstein is a composite portrait of both her father and her husband. After the trauma of Shelley's death, Mary returned to London in 1823 (where *Frankenstein* was already being staged) to look after her father and her surviving son, Percy Florence.

Though much courted (by women as well as men), she never remarried but lived quietly in retirement steadily publishing her later novels:

Valperga (1823), *The Last Man* (1826, also a science fiction novel set in a republican England in the twenty-first century), *The Fortunes of Perkin Warbeck* (1830, an historical romance), *Lodore* (1835), *Falkner* (1837), and a distinguished biographical collection, *Lives of the Most Eminent Literary and Scientific Men of France* (1837). She sent her son to Harrow, like Byron, and dedicated the remainder of her life to seeing him conventionally educated, happily married and safely settled on his country estate at Boscombe Down, Sussex, to be as much unlike his father Shelley as possible.

Brilliantly clever, shy, pale, painfully unexpressive in company, Mary Shelley hid a passionate nature that probably very few people except Godwin, Shelley and her friend Jane Williams (whose husband was also drowned in the *Ariel* disaster) ever really saw. Her half-sister Claire Clairmont called her 'a mixture of vanity and good nature'.

Her elusive character is oddly reflected in the history of her portraits. An early picture by Amelia Curran done in Rome (1819) was lent to Trelawny for safe-keeping, and subsequently lost in his wanderings. Drawings by Edward Williams done at Pisa for Shelley's birthday (1821) disappeared after the shipwreck. A striking portrait of 'an unknown woman' by John Stump (National Portrait Gallery, 1831), said to be Mary surrounded by her books and holding up a lover's locket assumed to contain Shelley's hair, has been consistently dismissed by modern art historians as unauthenticated, even though it corresponds closely to a contemporary description by Elizabeth Rennie:

> *If not a beauty, she was a most* lovable-*looking woman; with skin exquisitely fair, and expressive gray eyes; features delicate, yet of the style and proportion that have won the term 'aristocratic'; hair of light but bright brown, mostly silky in texture and luxuriant in profusion, which hung in long drooping ringlets over her colourless cheek, and gathered in a cluster behind, fell waveringly over her shoulders; a large, open forehead; white and well-moulded arms and hands. She was a degree under the middle height, and rather enclining to embonpoint.*

(Traits of Character, vol. 1, 1860)

Richard Rothwell's portrait, showing Mary as a much-subdued and evidently suffering older woman, was probably completed in 1840. Though the eyes are still full of tender intelligence, the great 'alabaster'

MARY SHELLEY
Richard Rothwell, exhibited 1840

shoulders suggest that she is turning into a monument. The curious
'flame-like' drapery in the background, revealed during cleaning at the
turn of the century, was said to represent Shelley's unappeased spirit
awaiting their reunion.

JOHN KEATS (1795–1821)

Though he became the epitome of the young, beautiful, doomed poet of late English Romanticism, Keats struck everyone who knew him with his tremendous energy, his robust good humour, and his zest for living. The son of a stables manager from the East End of London, he was built rather like a fly-weight boxer, short, stocky, with disproportionate broad shoulders and a strong, open face with a powerful, bony nose. Sensuous, highly intelligent, a lover of good claret and good company, he said poetry should be 'felt on the pulses'.

Apprenticed for four years to an apothecary, he applied in 1815 to study surgery at Guy's Hospital where he walked the wards and attended medical lectures, while reading widely in seventeenth- and eighteenth-century English literature. In 1816 he had the good fortune to meet Leigh Hunt, who published his sonnet 'On First Looking into Chapman's Homer' in the *Examiner* newspaper.

Poet, literary journalist and biographer, Leigh Hunt (1784–1859) edited *The Examiner* and kept open house for young writers and painters at his rambling establishment in Hampstead. He helped launch both Keats and Shelley in an influential series of articles 'On Young Poets' (1816), and later went to Italy to edit *The Liberal*, publishing work by Shelley, Byron and Hazlitt. He wrote a fine, gossipy *Autobiography* (1850), and was caricatured by Dickens as the cheerfully improvident and fawning Harold Skimpole in *Bleak House*.

Valuable friendships with Hazlitt, Lamb, B.R. Haydon, the young poet John Hamilton Reynolds, and Shelley (not altogether easy) quickly followed and helped Keats's work to develop with astonishing speed and confidence. He published a first volume of *Poems* in 1817, and his first extended work, *Endymion*, in 1818. Though scathingly attacked in *Blackwood's Edinburgh Magazine*, as the adolescent member of the

JAMES HENRY LEIGH HUNT
Samuel Laurence, *c.*1837

JOHN KEATS, William Hilton after Joseph Severn, *c.*1823

'Cockney School', he went on undaunted with his verse-epic *Hyperion*. During these hectic and exciting years he wrote a series of superb letters on poetry, many to his brothers George and Tom, and his sister Fanny, which contain his most influential ideas: Imagination as 'Negative Capability' (partly drawn from Coleridge), art as 'disinterested', style as 'fine excess', and life as 'a vale of Soul-making'. When Tom died of consumption, Keats moved to his friend Charles Armitage Brown's house on the edge of Hampstead Heath; their next-door neighbour was the eighteen-year-old Fanny Brawne with whom he fell passionately in love.

In the twelve months from September 1818, Keats produced an outpouring of major poetry which is unmatched in English: 'The Eve of St Agnes', 'Ode to a Nightingale', 'Ode on Melancholy', 'Ode to Psyche', 'Ode on a Grecian Urn', 'La Belle Dame sans Merci' (again partly inspired by Coleridge), 'Lamia', and the quintessential poem of Keatsian ripeness, 'To Autumn'. They were all published in July 1820, and Keats's future seemed assured. But that spring he had begun spitting up arterial blood (which as a medical student he instantly recognised as the symptom of consumption), and in September

JOHN KEATS
Charles Armitage Brown, 1819

he sailed for Italy with his friend Joseph Severn, hoping the southern climate might bring a remission from the fatal illness. Keats wrote no more poetry, and died in a tiny apartment above the Spanish Steps in Rome, in February 1821. Listening to the plashing Bernini fountain in the piazza below his window, he framed his own epitaph: 'here lies one whose name was writ in water.' His poetry has flowed out to generations of readers ever since.

Keats was often sketched by his friends Severn, Brown and Haydon (who also made a life-mask), and was perceptively observed by Hunt:

His shoulders were very broad for his size; he had a face in which energy and sensibility were remarkably mixed up, and eager power checked and made patient by ill-health. Every feature was at once strongly cut and delicately alive. If there was any faulty expression it was in the mouth which was not without something of a character of pugnacity. The face was rather long than otherwise … the chin was bold, the cheeks sunken; the eyes mellow and glowing, large dark and sensitive.

(Lord Byron and Some of His Contemporaries, 1828)

William Hilton's famous picture of Keats brooding over his manuscript book of poems, and perhaps foreseeing his own death, turns out to be posthumous. It is a careful amalgamation of several visual sources: Severn's ivory miniature (1819), Hilton's own chalk drawing, also done from life (1820), and a death-mask made in Rome (1821). It was actually painted as a souvenir for Keats's friend Richard Woodhouse, probably in 1823.

Joseph Severn also went to enormous pains to reconstruct a remembered image of Keats in the study at Wentworth Place, Hampstead, when he had just completed the 'Ode to a Nightingale' in spring 1819. Severn actually began it in Rome in autumn 1821, several months after Keats's death, and over two years added meticulous authenticating details: 'the room, the open window, the carpet and chairs are all exact portraits, even to the mezzotint portrait of Shakespeare given him by his old landlady in the Isle of Wight.' (*Letters*, 1859) In these works, Romantic portraiture has taken on a new emotional impulse, a conscious tribute to lost genius, a secular form of sacred iconography. They appear to be vividly realistic 'likenesses', but they are really pious memorials.

JOHN KEATS, Joseph Severn, 1821–3

JOHN CLARE (1793–1864)

❧

The last in a long line of eighteenth-century 'ploughboy' poets, Clare arrived in London from Northamptonshire in 1820 with the straw still clinging to his worsted jacket. He was the son of a farm-labourer from the village of Helpstone near Peterborough, and had taught himself to write poetry while working as a hedge-setter and lime-burner. Influenced by Crabbe and Goldsmith rather than Wordsworth, he brought a late flowering of the Romantic sensibility to a realistic knowledge of agricultural work and farming landscapes.

Clare's first book, *Poems Descriptive of Rural Life and Scenery* (1820), was accepted for publication by Keats's bookseller, Taylor and Hessey of Fleet Street, with an advance of £100. It sold out within two months, and Clare became the darling of the London literary season, meeting Hazlitt, Hunt, Lamb, and Coleridge. It was followed by *The Village Minstrel* (1821), *The Shepherd's Calendar* (1827) and *The Rural Muse* (1835). Clare's poetry, with exquisite and earthy observations of the natural world (dung as well as dew-drops), is suffused by a sense of loss and an awareness of hardships, and the unfeeling cruelty of the great landlords. His own life became increasingly disturbed and unhappy as the sudden vogue for his poetry declined, and in 1837 he was admitted to an insane asylum at Epping. Though married to a faithful wife, Martha Turner, he came to believe he was living with his first, abandoned love, Mary Joyce. After escaping to rejoin Mary in 1841, he spent the rest of his life in Northampton General Asylum, continuing to pour out poetry that remained largely unpublished for many years. The full text of his Romantic satire, *The Parish*, was only published from a manuscript in Peterborough Museum in 1985.

When Clare first came to London at the age of twenty-seven, he was a thin wiry figure with long sideburns and a fine country bloom upon his cheeks. But his deep-set eyes and prominent cheek-bones already told of suffering and inner turmoils. The society writers gushed over his acute, natural sensitivity: 'What life in the eyes! What ardent thirst for excellence, and what flexibility and susceptibility to outward impression in the quivering lips!' (T.G. Wainewright, *The London Magazine*, 1821)

The editor Thomas Hood met him at a smart dinner party, nervously sipping a tankard of ale and shining 'verdantly' amidst the urban literati:

JOHN CLARE, William Hilton, 1820

'in his bright grass-coloured coat and yellow waistcoat (there are greenish stalks, too, under the table) he looks a very cowslip.' (*The London Magazine*, 1823) Hilton's moving portrait, which captures Clare's extraordinary mixture of innocence and painful anxiety, was commissioned by his publisher Taylor in the first flush of his fatal London celebrity of 1820.

THE INVISIBLE ROMANTICS

❦

It is safe to say that not one person in a thousand will ever have heard of Mary Tighe (1772–1810), read a line of her poetry, or previously seen her entrancing picture (which is actually a miniature on ivory, no bigger than a beer mat). Yet in 1805 she published a major Romantic poem in six cantos, *Psyche*, which went through five English editions, and then appeared in Philadelphia. She was read by Keats, who enjoyed her and then felt he had grown out of her: 'Mrs Tighe and James Beattie once delighted me – now I see through them and can find nothing in them – or weakness – and yet how many they will still delight!' (*Letters*, 1819) Yet like many others he was obviously influenced by her work, with its high sense of romance and melancholy visions of solitude.

Mary Tighe represents the most notable absence from the Romantic Circle: that of the many gifted women writers of the period, well-known to their contemporaries, but strangely ignored by modern literary studies. For those who had other social roles to play – prominent actresses like Mary Robinson, mistresses of the great like Lady Caroline Lamb, sisters of famous men like Mary Lamb and Dorothy Wordsworth, or literary wives like Mary Shelley or (irony of ironies) Mary Wollstonecraft – history or the collective male memory has been more gallant and hospitable.

But the others have become cruelly invisible, and even the impartial archives of the National Portrait Gallery retain scant visual records because so few portraits were commissioned or bequeathed by their friends, lovers, husbands, or publishers. There is one drawing of the Jacobin novelist Elizabeth Inchbald (1753–1821); one mezzotint of the self-educated poet Ann Yearsley (1756–1808) who supported herself with a daily milk-round in Bristol; one stipple engraving of the poet Charlotte Smith (1749–1806) of whom Wordsworth calmly wrote: 'A Lady to whom English verse is under greater obligations than are likely to be either acknowledged or remembered'. (*Letters*, 1835) And no known portrait at all of the working-class poet from Kendal in the Lake District, Isabella Lickbarrow (even her dates are unknown).

Neither Mary Tighe's maiden name, nor the place of her birth, nor the circumstances of her life, are recorded in the archives. It appears that she was unhappily married to an Anglo-Irish Member of Parliament, had no children, and died from consumption at the age of thirty-eight. She wrote a novel, but it was never published. When Wordsworth's bookseller Longman reissued *Psyche* in 1811 (the edition that Keats read) he placed on the title page which I now have open in front of me: 'Poems by the late Mrs Henry Tighe'. That was the extent of her Romantic Circle.

MARY TIGHE, attributed to John Comerford, *c.*1810, after George Romney, 1795

List of Illustrations